Broken Bones

By

Kenneth T. Burles

ROURKE PRESS, INC.
VERO BEACH, FLORIDA 32964

Printed in the United States of America.

Library of Congress Cataloging-in-Publication Data

Burles, Kenneth T., 1946-
    Broken bones / Kenneth T. Burles.
        p.   cm. — (Learning about your health)
Includes index.
Summary: Explains how and why bones break, tells how such injuries are treated and how they may be prevented.
    ISBN 1-57103-253-3
    1. Bones—Wounds and injuries—Juvenile literature.. 2. Fractures in
children—Juvenile literature. [1. Bones—Wounds and injuries. 2. Fractures.] I. Title. II. Series.
RD101.B937   1998
617.1'5—dc21   98-22379
                                                                                         CIP
                                                                                         AC

Photographs: Cover, pp.8, 15, © Digital Stock; pp. 5, 13, 16, 27, © RubberBall Productions; pp. 7, 21, 25, © Adobe Systems Incorporated; pp. 18, 23, © PhotoDisc.

Illustrations by Paul Calderon.

Contents

Crack!

You are riding your bicycle home from school. A car turns the corner in front of you. You put on the brakes. Your bicycle skids. You are falling over. You put out your hand to break your fall. You hear a crack and feel a pain in your wrist. You may have broken a bone.

You can break a
bone from falling
off your bicycle.

What is a Fracture?

A broken or cracked bone is called a fracture (**frak**-sure). Fractures happen when too much pressure (**presh**-sure) is put on a bone. Your body weight put too much pressure on your bone when you fell. Bones will stretch, but only so much. Then they break or crack.

Children's bones stretch more than those of adults. The older you get, the less elastic (e-**lass**-tick) your bones become. That is why many older people are careful not to fall.

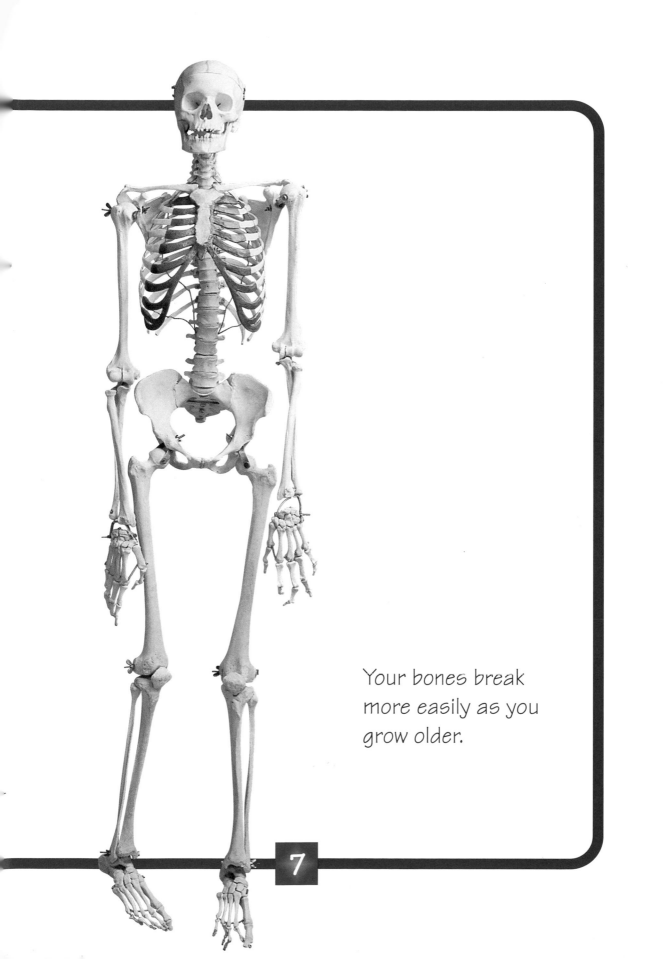

Your bones break
more easily as you
grow older.

Some types of fractures

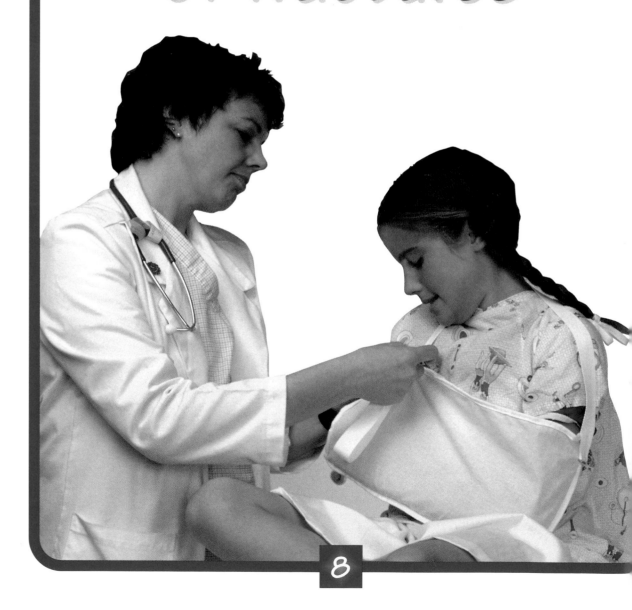

Transverse (transe-**verse**)	At right angle to the bone
Oblique (o-**bleak**)	At an angle to the bone
Spiral (**spy**-rul)	From a twisted force
Comminuted (coe-**min**-yut-ed)	Shattered, splintered, or crushed
Hairline (**hair**-line)	A crack but not separated
Green-stick (**green**-stik)	Partly broken like bending a green branch
Compression (come-**presh**-shun)	Crushed bone
Stress (**stress**)	Stress on the bone at the same place again and again
Undisplaced (**un**-dis-placed)	Pieces of bone remain in normal positions
Displaced (dis-**placed**)	Pieces of bone are not in normal positions

How Do Bones Break?

There are many ways a bone can break. All fractures are either simple or compound. In a simple or closed fracture, the bone does not break the skin. In a compound or open fracture, the bone breaks the skin. You may be able to see the bone. An open fracture can become **infected** (in-**feckt**-ed). It must be clean. Call a doctor right away.

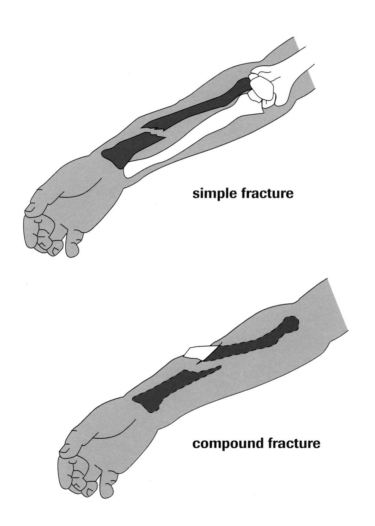

simple fracture

compound fracture

When Do Bones Break?

Children break bones when playing. It could be from falling out of a tree. It could be from a crash on the soccer field. Many people fall when they ski. A bad fall may mean a broken ankle or leg. Most fractures occur in the wrist, arm, ankle, or lower leg. Most fractures are not serious.

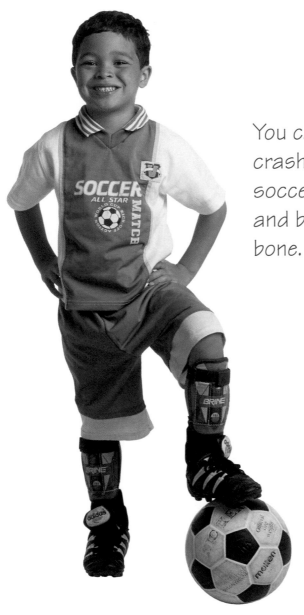

You can crash on the soccer field and break a bone.

How Do I Know If I Broke a Bone?

I t is not always easy to know if a bone is fractured. Sometimes a doctor cannot tell by looking at the patient (**pay-**shunt). Ask these questions:

- **Does it hurt?**

- **Can you put pressure on it?**

- **Is there swelling?**

- **Is there bruising (brews-ing)?**

- **Has the bone moved from the normal position?**

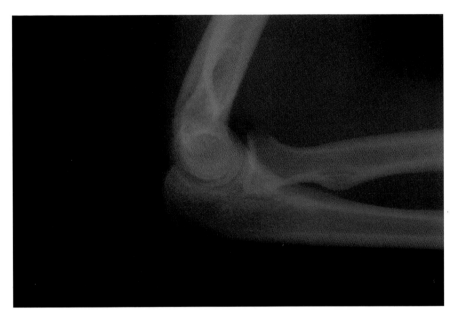

The doctor takes an x ray, or picture, of your bone to see if it is broken.

Once you get to a doctor's office, an X ray will show what is wrong with the bone. An X ray does not hurt. It is like taking a picture of the bone through the skin.

What Do I Do?

You are playing with a friend. She has an **accident** (**ak**-sid-ent). You think a bone is broken. Here is what you should do:

It is important to know how we can help our friends and others when there is an accident.

- Keep her calm.

- Do not move the injured part.

- Put ice on the injury to reduce swelling.

- Do not straighten the bones.

- Raise the injured part above the heart to prevent swelling.

- For a leg injury make a splint to support the leg.

- Wrap a blanket or towel around the injury. Tie a stick on the padding. The leg cannot bend now.

- For an arm injury make a sling.
  Take a triangle of cloth. Fold the arm to an L shape. Rest the arm in the cloth. Tie the ends of the cloth behind the neck.

- Ask an adult for medicine to relieve any pain.

- Take her to a doctor.

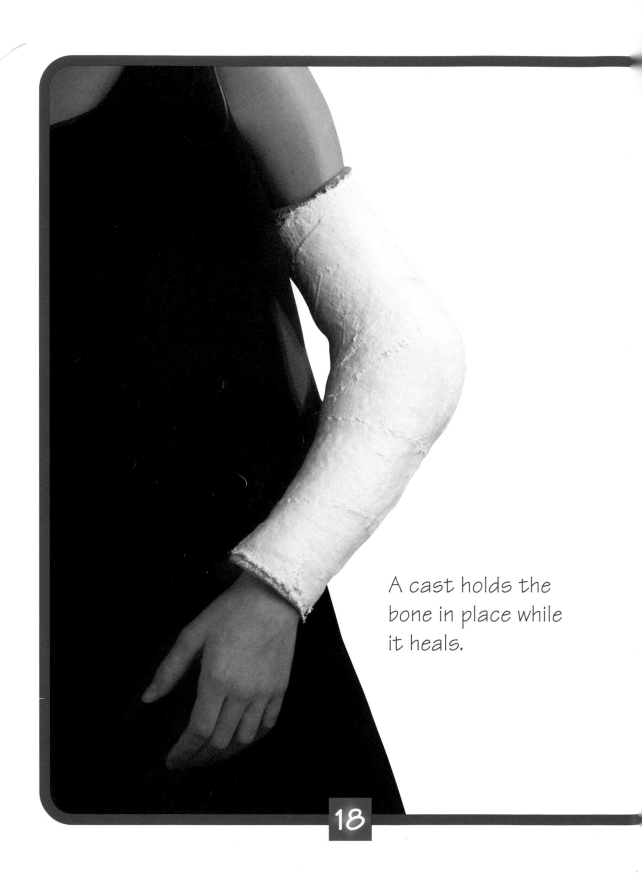

A cast holds the bone in place while it heals.

What Will the Doctor Do?

The doctor will look at the injury and take an X ray. Then the bone must be put in the normal position, or set, so it can heal. The doctor's hands feel the ends of the bone move into place. A cast will hold the pieces of bone in place while they heal, or grow together.

A cast is often made of plaster (plass-tur) and fiberglass (fi-burr-glass). The plaster takes the shape of the arm or leg. The fiberglass holds the plaster and protects (pro-tekts) it. Some casts are made of plastic. They can be filled with air like a balloon that wraps around an arm or leg.

While It Heals

It is important to keep the injured part elevated to reduce swelling. If the injured limb swells, the cast will become too tight.

Sometimes you cannot put weight on a broken ankle or leg. Then you must learn to walk on **crutches** (**kruch**-es). The crutches hold up your body so you do not put any weight on the broken leg.

It will take at least 6 to 8 weeks for the fracture to heal. Then it takes four more weeks until you are ready to go back to normal activities.

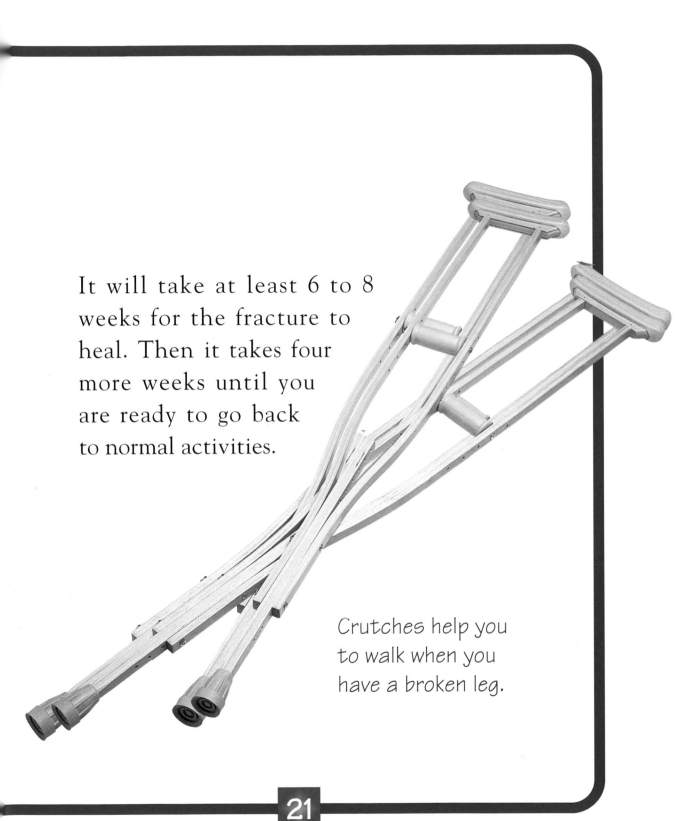

Crutches help you to walk when you have a broken leg.

How Serious Is It?

If you are lucky, you might have a **sprain** (**sprayn**) not a fracture. A sprain hurts immediately and continues to be painful. A sprain is an injury of the **ligaments** (**lig**-ah-mints), the elastic band that holds the bones in place. Sprains usually are caused by a quick twist. A hard twist of the ankle can cause a sprain. An ankle sprain is a common sports injury.

You also might have a **dislocation** (dis-

low-**kay**-shun). You can dislocate a shoulder, a finger, or a toe. Ligaments hold the bones together at the joint, such as the shoulder. When they stretch too much, the bone slips out of the joint or dislocates. The doctor first relaxes the **muscles** (**muss**-suls). Then he can pull the bone until it slides back into the joint.

Serious Fractures

The most serious fractures are those of the **spinal vertebrae** (**spy**-nul **ver**-tah-bray). The vertebrae run up your back and protect the spinal cord. The spinal cord carries the nerves from your brain to your body. If the vertebrae are fractured, they can cut the spinal cord. That can **paralyze** (**pair**-a-lies) a person. A paralyzed person cannot move his hands or feet or control his body below the cut.

The actor Christopher Reeve fractured vertebrae in his neck when he fell from a horse. He is now in a wheelchair. He has no control over his body below his neck. Much research is being done to try and find ways to heal the injured spinal cord. These fractures usually happen in automobile accidents, athletic injuries, or falls from high places.

A person who is paralyzed needs to use a wheelchair to get around.

You Can Prevent Broken Bones

You can make your bones stronger with exercise. Athletes avoid many broken bones because they lift weights and exercise. Their bones are stronger and can take a hard blow. They also learn to fall properly.

Many bones break because of carelessness. If you play a sport, you should be supervised. You also should learn to play the sport properly. You should not try to do more than you know how. Protection is also important. A helmet protects your head when you ride a bicycle, roller blade, or play football. Pads on your elbows, knees, and shins are a good idea if you roller blade.

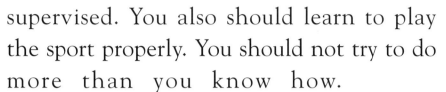

It is important to protect your head and knees while rollerblading.

Glossary

accident (**ak**-sid-ent)- something you do not expect to happen. A fall from a tree is an accident.

bruise (**brews**) - a dark spot under the skin; an injury makes blood collect under the skin.

cast- something a doctor puts on a broken leg or arm so it cannot move while it heals.

crutches (**kruch**-es) - two sticks made of metal or wood with handles to support your body. You cannot put pressure on a broken leg so you walk with crutches.

dislocate (dis-**low**-kate) - when a bone slips out of a joint it is dislocated.

elastic (e-**lass**-tick)- something that stretches or bends is elastic. A rubber band is elastic.

fiberglass (**fi**-burr-glass)- a material you mix that can be molded and dries like plastic.

fracture (**frak**-sure)- a cracked or broken bone is called a fracture.

infect (in-**fekt**)- when bacteria gets in a wound it becomes infected.

injure (**in**-jur) - to hurt yourself or someone else

ligament (**lig**-ah-mint) - elastic tissue that holds the bones together.

28

muscles (**muss**-suls) - a body tissue that gets bigger with pressure; muscles make you strong.

paralyze (**pair**-a-lies) - when a person cannot control his body. This can be because the spinal cord has been cut in an accident.

patient (**pay**-shunt) - a person who goes to the doctor is a patient.

plaster (**plass**-turr) - a material you mix that can be molded and then dries in shape.

pressure (**presh**-sure) - to apply force. When you push your hand against something you apply pressure.

protect (pro-**tekt**) - to keep something from being hurt or damaged.

set - place broken bones in their normal position so they heal

spinal (**spy**-nul) - anything about the spine; the spine runs up the middle of your back.

splint - a piece of wood or metal that keeps a body part from moving.

sprain (**sprayn**) - an injury to the ligaments.

swell - to become large after an injury. When you sprain an ankle it swells.

vertebrae (**ver**-tah-bray) - the bones that run up the middle of your back.

For More Information

Children's Healthwatch from Mayo Clinic. http://healthfront.com

Grolier Encyclopedia of Science and Technology. Danbury, CT: Grolier Educational Corporation, 1994.

Health Infopark. http://www.merck.com

Kingfisher Children's Encyclopedia. New York: Kingfisher Books, 1992.

Raintree Steck-Vaughn Illustrated Science Encyclopedia. Austin, TX: Steck-Vaughn, 1997.

Rourke's World of Science Encyclopedia. Vero Beach, FL: Rourke Corporation, Inc., 1998.

The World Book Encyclopedia. Chicago: World Book, Inc., 1998.

Index